The
AKnowledgeMEnt

By:

Aneski Ana Kemsit

Printed in the United States of America

First Printing, 2026

Aneski Ana Kemsit
4authorsaup@gmail.com

Dedicated to
Thomasina Shanee' Redmond

Table Of Contents

Forward

To acknowledge is to accept the existence of Truth.
Not the polished truth.
Not the half-truth.
Not the conveniently omitted one.
But the naked kind—the kind that remembers what we are before the world told us *who* to be.

As beings of light, we've come to have a spiritual experience in a human incarnation. And those of us who arrived in this lifetime as women carry the voice of Wisdom within us.

Somewhere in the HIStory of patriarchal paradigms and smoking mirrors, the world seems to have forgotten this Universal Truth. More devastating still, we—the keepers of Wiisdom—have forgotten ourselves.

Over centuries of society's neglect, disrespect, and the unwillingness to protect us ,we learned to doubt what we carry, to wait our turn, to outsource our intuitive knowing for validation. We forgot we were created from a knowing that transcends intellect. A power that surpasses physical strength. A peace that trumps human understanding. We have forgotten that we as women are Wisdom walking.

This is what *The AKnowledgeMEnt* does. In the pages to follow, Aneski Ana Kemset writes with courage—not only the courage to speak her own truth but the courage to give other Black women permission to do the same. These poems do not ask to be approved. They declare acceptance. They say: I see what I am. I name it. I claim it.

May these words meet you where you are and remind you of what you truly are.

Tiffany C. Ginyard

To the Reader

How can something be acknowledged if it doesn't have a name?

Well, I have many names. One given to me at birth and others gained as endearments. I have even earned a few entitlements in the time of my existence, as well.

I have awakened in this body for over four decades and yet everyday still feels like an introduction. The person I have become is a new embodiment that I fully embrace with anxiousness and ambition, only to transform even more, as time goes on. Nonetheless, I am confident this is who I am supposed to be, and I am living in my true purpose.

But my purpose would be null and void, if it were not for you, the reader. I am so thankful for your presence because the words in this book, represent the challenges I have overcome from the beginning of my conception until now; and through them I intend to develop a connection that is genuinely based on the human need for acceptance, accountability, and action; all three work in tandem as self-validation.

How can something be acknowledged if it doesn't have a name?

Well, I have a name. My name is Aneski Ana Kemsit.
Aneski literally means "she belongs to me."

CERTIFICATE OF EXPRESSION

<u>SHE</u>

All of a sudden,
he was hatin',
while she was
still huggin'.
She was too
busy lovin'
all his bullshit.
She stayed
because she
loved him,
but that
wasn't enough.
Ain't that
some bullshit?
She wanted him
to stay forever.
He stayed long
enough to quit.
Because her value
wasn't in her worth,
it was in her
full-time benefits.

She was blind.
In her eyes,
he told no lies.
He only hid
the truth.
Miscommunication,

create misunderstandins.
Her motives
became misconstrued.
Her intentions
were unforgiven.
His excuse
for his misuse,
and the reason
why he used to,
but no longer do
all he did before
the honeymoon.

Ego trips
sail past
partnerships.
Legal contracts
make legit,
the fantasies and
broken promises,
unforeseen
circumstances
a commitment
with a twist.
She made vows
to stay forever,
but forever
didn't exist.
Her side effects

from past trauma
kept her bondage,
kept her sick.
He was her
trigger,
semi-automatic.
Now she's pleadin'
self-defense.
She realized
his mentality
was a trap,
not a reality.
She look back
on how she
sacrificed
her sanity
for loyalty.
A martyr in
a marriage,
she moves on
with no regrets.
The broken pieces
are scattered
like the memories
she now yearns
to forget....
But how can she,
when she
is me.

QUESTIONS

What is the answer?
There are somethings
I think I may
never know.
It seems as if
I spend countless hours
searching for something
I never lost,
and may never find.
(Much like my car keys,
after a long night
and a lot of wine.)
Nevertheless, I look
for it with hope
and maybe that is
the key to finding
the answers to the
questions, constantly
bombarding my mind.
I feel such a need
to inquire about everything,
and no nothing of what
I am in search for.
It's probably not
hidden under much,
just some light rubble,
a thought or two,

or maybe a mound
of meaningful knowledge,
all tattered on my brain
like ink drawn on
the canvas of my skin.
Pondering the idea
of knowing what
no one else knows,
not even me.
I'd let my
inquisitive moments
pass me by,
if I weren't filled
with curiosity.
I am ashamed to
lack philosophy,
intellect, logic,
and most of all wisdom;
for among them all,
it is the most desired.
I have no peace
because I do not
have the answer
which holds the key
to the age-old question,
"Why am I even here?"

Despite the melodic
tone of my mother's
lovely voice,
constantly reminding me
I am forever loved
and adored
as a gift from above,
it doesn't ease me
because the truth is
the answer to all
my life questions
is obviously a mystery
only to be discovered
in eternity.
How many lonely
nights wondering
why do I feel like
love has passed
me by,
yet somehow managing
to still hold on to
what little love
I have inside?
Just another subject
that troubles the neurotic
sensors in my mind.

Curiosity has always
been a sensation,
not so much a temptation,
just a ball of confusion,
disrupting the harmony
of me,
myself,
and I.

<u>SPEAK</u>

Speak!
Let life
flow from
your tongue
like lyrics flow
through a song.
Make music
with your words.
Be God.
Create a world
and fill it
with peace,
harmony,
and love.
Arrange them
in the universe,
intricately place
them like
celestial beings
above.
Spew fire
at those
who have proven
to be enemies
because words
cut sharper
than a two
edge sword.

Therefore,
speak nice
when addressing
me and know
you have
been warned.

Talk!
Open up
your mouth
and speak;
forming words to
circulate
intellectual
conversations,
which will have
a positive,
cognitive effect.
Curse others
with knowledge,
having been
educated
through experiences
and graduated from
"The School of
Hardknocks",
where there's
no need

for a
college degree
and forget English
because
it is not
your native tongue.
Let your lectures
be about history.
Tell the tales
that have been
forgotten
because they
were rewritten
by white men
with a pad
and a pen.

Shout!
Speak loud
and proud.
Squander not
for hypocrites,
nay sayers,
backstabbers,
no-good doers
and liar - liars;
let them all
burn like
forest fires

Let the truth
reign!
May it ring
louder than
an alarm.
Too long
Have our
voices gone
unheard,
unappreciated,
undermined,
and buried
over time.
Our images
have been
regurgitated
and rehearsed
in a way
we don't even
recognize.
We will say,
"Nigga Please",
when the
wise ones
take the time
to remind
us we are
Kings and Queens.

No one wants
to say
these things
except me
and now you,
So do
as I say....
Speak Truth!

LET GO

Let it go!
Three simple words.
Three syllables.
Let it go.

Let it ring
in your ear
and hear what
you must reveal
to yourself,
not just because
they want you to,
and not because
the date on
the calendar is new,
but because you
deserve a better you...
So, LET that shit GO!

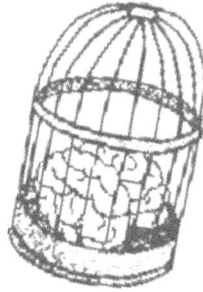

I know you're hurt
and they made you cry.
I would not
stand here
and lie,
and say I
haven't had
hell of sleepless nights.

But eventually
I had to see
the only thing
that was keeping me
from going to sleep
was me.
I realized
in order to
pick up and go
I had to pick
my head up
and LET that shit GO.

I see you're lonely.
I know you need help.
I would not
stand here
and lie,
and say I never
had a knife
in my chest.
But eventually
I had to accept
what I allowed
had a consequence,
and in doing so
I elevated

my confidence.
I realized
in order to grow
I had to pick
my head up
and LET that shit GO!

Let it go!
Three simple words.
Three syllables.
LET it GO!

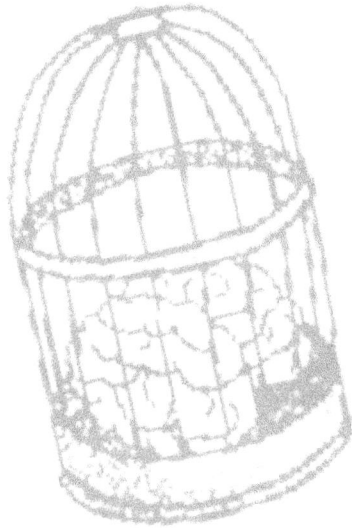

THE FINISH

I can see you
pushing forward,
enduring upon
your brow,
the compulsion
of knowing
we're cheering
you on.
I can hear the crowd,
"Hip hip hooray!"
You've made it
through another day.
Therapy is not
for the weak,
Therefore,
you show up
week after week.

The counselor
is asking the doctor
who is practicing
by the textbook,
standards which never
really prepare them
for what really happens
beyond the classroom.

The diagnosis is in.
That's when the action begins.
Lights, bright in a room.
Camera, needles, pills,
straight jacket...
medical tools used
to do what professionals
have been trained to do.
Test after test, only
to realize the answer
to the true question,
resides inside.

It's not about the win
because whether
you're first or last,
you better celebrate!
Everyone is a champion
because this is life,
not a race.
It requires no running,
no walking, no jogging
yet you gotta keep your pace.
But it does require
a ton of strength,
a pound of endurance,
and a teaspoon of assurance,
which can easily be applied
with a dab of hope
and a drop of faith.

The fans in the stands
consist of family and friends,
I'd say more "A ones"
than "Day ones",
and frienimies, at least.
Could be rumors?
I don't know.
So, save your steak sauce
for the real beef.
Shout out to the ride or dies,
who never gave up.
And shout out to the prayer warriors
who never got up.
This is for us.
Though there is no
medal at the end,
only a prognosis,
you know you're
going to win,
your will to live
a healthy life
is your only motive.
So, you're fearless and committed.
You push yourself
past unimaginable limits.
Each day is a challenge for you,
but you press on
because you know,
it's not how you begin...
it's all about the finish.

PRETTY GURL

I never was
treated like
a pretty gurl.
Maybe cuz
my hair was short
wit natural curls,
not long
and luscious;
never was into
fake hair,
fake nails,
didn't care much
about makeup,
like eyeshadow
and blush;
nor plump
cherry colored lips.
I wasn't very
particular
bout tight jeans,
in fact I let
my pants hang
off my hips.
I'm pretty sure
I could fox trot
in some heels,
if I didn't bop

pass a bunch of
fine ass boys,
who never whistled,
and so I
never stopped.
Even tho he
was among Dem,
Yea him...
I liked a lot.
But never
was I brave
enough to
put him on
da spot.
Mostly cuz
I never was
treated like
a pretty gurl,

In a world
where fair
complexion and
flawless skin
had me dislikin'
da dark,
like a shadow
covered in
jokes and
wise cracks

bout bein black.
Pointy fingers
and snide remarks
sparked flames
like fire crackers.
Fist fights
led to scars
more hidden
than revealed,
much deeper
still not healed,
Prolly cuz...
I never was
treated like
a pretty gurl.

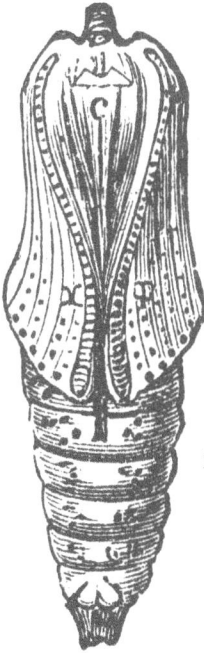

Even tho
my Daddy
constantly
tells Me
how beautiful
I am,
it never seemed
to mean much
until I heard
it from
another man.
Even a princess

desires a knight
over a king,
and I desired
a man
who would
tell me
such things.
Life lessons
left me
vexed and
it taught me
all about
my lack of
self-esteem.

Now I don't
need you
or anyone
to tell me
I'm a
pretty gurl.
I look
in the mirror
and rub my
fingers through
my tight curls.
I oil my
copper tone skin

knowing beauty
only shines
from within;
bein humble
and upliftin,'
unitin'
and invitin';
a flower that
has blossomed
from the
finest seed,
no longer waitin'
on the
compliments
of this
ugly world.
Now I
tell myself
constantly...
I'm a pretty gurl!

CERTIFICATE OF VALIDATION

<u>BELONGS TO</u>

This book
belongs to the one
who seeks acknowledgment,
who desires to
belong to so much
more than family,
who yearns to
fulfill so much more
than a simple timeline,
whose destiny
belongs to the prophecies
of our faithful ancestors,
them who stayed on
hands and knees, thanking
the most high for daily
grace and mercy, which
belongs to the one
who has taken
that one moment
to appreciate life
just as it is.

True love
belongs to every
living being, as well as
the wisdom to obtain

the riches and desires
of the heart,
although this knowledge
belongs to the culture,
the education system
belongs to our foes,
and our faith
belongs to those
who choose to seek
Gods face, only
to find themselves,
hoping their tribulations
will guide the way,
as if to be a lamp
illuminating the lives
of others with hope.

That same hope
belongs to our communities,
so the next generation
can confidently lead
with courage,
changing and breaking
the chains that imprison
the minds of our youth
because the future
belongs to the ones
who nurture the young,
allowing legacies to

become fables, and creating
stories to guide the righteous
along the path
to glory, for God
belongs to the one
who believes in
their own destiny,
and they will live forever...

for death only
belongs to those
who fear eternity.

THROUGH ALL ETERNITY

All my life I've been
told to work hard.
If you want it, go get it
but it will cost you
blood, sweat, tears,
heartache, and scars.
Why is it I must bleed
to achieve a status
stripped from me?
I see centuries of phenomenal
women leaving legacies
all the while fighting
through all eternity
to remain a Queen.

Is it she that sees
life and thinks
selfless enough
to carry a seed?
Nine months her body
change before her
eyes.
No more slender hips.
Her ankles swollen
like her thighs.
She can only eat this
and drink that,
feeding herself
insecurities,

as a fetus occupies
her womb,
soon to be
a newborn baby.
Yes, she bleeds
to achieve
a position,
Mommy,
fighting all
through eternity
to remain
a Queen.

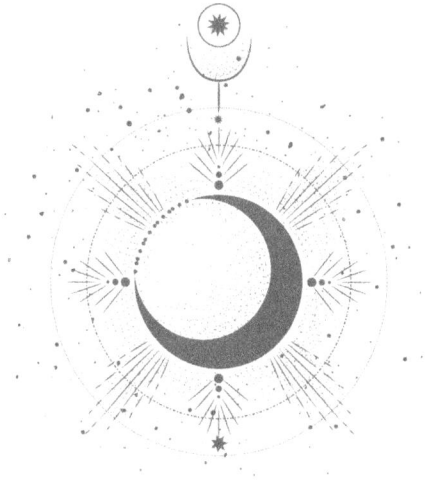

THE QUEEN'S CAKE

So high and mighty
sit the rich,
those who have crowned
themselves kings and queens.
Carnivorous connoisseurs
who have spent
centuries colonizing,
creating countries,
conquering natives,
and incorporating
natural resources.
Mutated offspring
of our purest bloodlines,
once isolated,
but somehow
educated and freed,
only to ostracize
the very Angel of Light
that chose to grace them
from their ignorance.
And now they have
the audacity
to stand over
those who have
endured the pain
of war, disease, famine,
whips and chains
with their nose turned

to the sky, as if to say,
"LET THEM EAT CAKE!"

Fuck Juneteenth!
Am I really to be
grateful for the
recognition of the signing
of documentation
to reroute slavery?
The shackles of
my great grandparents
were never loosened,
but only lessened
to a degree that
focused solely on the
cultural castration
and industrial uprising
of this corporation,
nicknamed a nation,
a.k.a. "Home of the Free".

Fuck King Day!
Am I to constantly
remind our future
that physical castration
won't be enough
to keep our people
from violently rising up,
with fist of fury,

beating down our oppressor,
to reclaim the land
we toiled on until
the day when that
sweet chariot would
swing low and take
our ancestors' home?
What sense does it make
to march up MLK Boulevard,
grand bands and flag girls,
stomp and twirl,
while the Republicans
can march right up
to the doors of the
White House,
kick it in,
vandalize and minimize
the very independence
declared for all citizens,
and literally march right out?
Ironically,
we grace this landmark
with a speech that constantly
leaves our people
in suspense,
as we continue
to turn the other cheek.

Fuck the twenty-eight days
used to remind us
we will always be
remembered as slaves!
Receiving less than deserved,
the list of colored people
who have contributed to
the accolades that
"make America great"
in the first place.
Our expertise exceeded
those considered to be
forefathers, the first
slave masters who paved
the way, establishing
a wicked line of defense
as justification for why
the ten commandments
do not apply to lawmakers
nor members of the clergy.

I can't be satisfied
with just cake!
Stereotyped to be a sucker
for festivities.
Throwing parties
every birthday
holiday, holy day.

and days we never celebrated
prior to the days
they raided the tombs
of the pharaohs,
the high priest and
keepers of the key.
Robbed of our nationality.
Assumed to accept
the hypocritical crumbs
of society, strategically
arranged to give us
just the bare minimum.
Any knowledge
we lack as a people
these days,
is shame on those
who are woke.
My despise for the crust
surrounding the lies
of this American apple pie
has caused me
to be unsatisfied
with this slice of heaven
offered to me by
the color of my
skin at birth.

I refuse to stay silent!
I speak the truth.
Are we hoping
the sweet morsels
of Uncle Sam's
delicate dessert
would make up for not
having a whole meal?

Blessed be the grace
that was said over
the stench of hog maws
and chitterlings.
Masters trash fed many
like two fish and
five loaves of bread.
Yet, my soul is still hungry
and I have made peace
with my destiny.

I will starve
before I eat the cake
like Annie Mae.
An indecent gesture
meant to emphasize

our insignificance
with a "Memorial Day".
No matter how fluffy
the buttercream icing might be,
every layer of disrespect
still taste bitter to me.
The ribbon dressing and
candy pearls won't hide
their heinous history.
And besides...
sugar coated bullshit
has never been
my cup of tea.

THE ELEPHANT IN THE ROOM

I have the right
to remain silent,
yet I have broken
no law with my words.
Am I not by
definition a citizen?
According to the
first amendment,
have I not the
right to be heard?

This democracy
is hypocrisy!
It's absolutely absurd.
The irony...independent
but not free to speak,
innocent yet already
guilty by decent,
systematically stripped,
still we steady
find ourselves
on some type
of plantation.
And it matters not,
how many ratifications,
there is no justification

for them who profit
from a bill drafted
to incorporate this nation
at my people's expense.

Uncle Sam has fattened
his pockets from the
silence of sacrificial lambs,
only to victim shame
when a peaceful protest
turns into a riot.
I may be bias,
but I do believe our
suffering has been
undermined
because it seems
the bottom line
is don't speak
unless spoken too.
And how when the
first amendment now
applies to me too?
Thanks to the fourteenth.
By the way,
let me show
some gratitude.

And yes,
that's sarcasm
at its best,
non the less,
I feel it is my duty
as a citizen to
exercise my right
to express.
Despite anything I say
will be used against me,
I am convinced
I am to be vigilant
and choose when
it is best to say less,
But I am a vigilante,
so I must say more.
To be blessed
with this gift
would be too
sinful to ignore.
I promise you,
if speaking one's
mind was a crime,
I'd walk the green mile
before I 'd walk
a straight line
because this democracy
is a hypocrisy;

and if someone is
gonna say it,
might as well be
someone brown
skinned like me.

O say can't you see?
They want us to
go down
without a fight,
but I ain't
goin down
because I know
my civil rights.
And I believe
our oppressors
have earned a
tongue lashing,
at least,
for every ancestor
that's been beaten
and treated like
a dog on a leash.
Just as sure enough
as I stand,
cuffed,
Miranda Rights
read to me.

I have the right
to remain silent
But I won't!
See they can
take our freedom
but they can't
take our freedom
of speech!

Now I said it...
and I'll say it again...

(In protest)
This democracy is hypocrisy!
This democracy is hypocrisy!
This democracy is hypocrisy!

WEN DA YELLIN' STOPS

Such profanity...
I heard daddy call
mommy a bitch,
after she called him
a dog ass nigga
and said he wasn't shit!
Cuz she'd been robbin'
Peter to pay Paul
witout suckin' dick.
She even labeled him
a corner boy,
pushin' pills,
hand to hand
pitchin' in front
da corner store.
She really dug
in his shit.
Her hand extended.
Her palm opened,
hopin' he'd
get da hint.
Gettin' rich
or die tryin'
hadn't earned him
fifty-cent.

She yelled,
"Yo, where da bread at?"

If money wasn't funny
den she wouldn't
be so pissed.
Totin' her home
on her back,
a tortoise, so to say.
Da world wouldn't
be on her shoulders,
if daddy wasn't
always away,
out entertainin'
da ones dat stroll pass,
battin' dey eyes
and shakin' dey ass.
He never cared
to stop and ask
how many lonely
nights she spent
prayin' he wouldn't
fall back into da
hands of da man
and have his freedom
taken by da government.

Mommy didn't want
it to be over,
despite bein' done,
and dats how da whole

argument begun.
She tried to stay
calm and sit
through da lies,
while Daddy
screamed to da top
of his lungs,
no matter how hard
she cried.
Daddy was bein toxic.
Slammin doors and
throwin' things.
Mommy got defensive
yet she still
tried to maintain.
She could hear
da devil clear
for her anger
was fueled by pain;
sick and tired of his
excuses for bein late.
She already ignored
how he came
and straight took
a shower.
smellin' like fried fish
and baby powder.

Automatic flag on da play!
Mommy no longer could
keep her demons away.

Da way Daddy
bent da truth
was a shot at da
vows she agreed to
wen she said, "I do."
Da camel's back broke
and Mommy slapped
Daddy's face.
Suddenly blood was all
Daddy could taste.

Wen da yellin' stopped,
dats wen da
beatin's begin.
Fist fights all night.
Everybody loses
and nobody wins.
A vicious cycle,
again and again.
What I witnessed
had me questionin'
what makes
a good girl go bad,
and what
makes a man,
a man.

RENT IS DUE

Dere's a notice on da door.
Did you see it?

Cuz I didn't notice
for it's been so many notices
out dere before,
you wouldn't believe it.
For some reason da
landlord thinks it's treason
if I pay my rent after
da fifth, so by da fifteenth
he's steady posting
notes on my door,
and I don't even read'em.

Cuz I don't need dem!
Its obvious, RENT IS DUE!

At da beginning of
every month every
responsible adult knows
it's time to pay up...
cuz RENT IS DUE!
Now you can cry.and
complain 'til you're blue
But nuffin changes da fact
Deres a cost to be da boss
And da head nigga in charge

seems to be you.

That's why I ain't got time
to sit and chit chat 'bout
who's sleepin' wit who,
who's skinny and who's fat,
who ain't got no job and
whose baby daddy is dat.
My bills are piled high
and dey da only racks
I got on deck.
With just enough chump
change to stay in debt.
Tuh...You ain't gotta wonder
what I'm doin' or where I'm at.
It's obvious.
I'm chasing da bag.
I can't even drag.
And wen I do,
my pockets wish I never had.
'Cuz now it's overtime
and now my eyes are
da ones carryin' da bags.
But don't you judge me
I'm sure your shit ain't
always been lovely.
And when it ain't,
it's dem sanctified saints
spreading rumors from door to door.

Just remember, I only heard it...
I never said you was a whore.

Anyways, what you here for?
You just standing' dere
like you ain't neva
been here before.
I know you read
da notice on da door.
Da one dat say
RENT IS DUE...

If you did,
you was bein' nosey,
and I'd mind my business,
if I was you.

12 O' CLOCK

Da son has risen.
I'm up, like dat bright star
in da sky, I shine.
I check da weather.
Clear skies.I'm outside.
I get dressed. I'm impressed.
My adrenaline is high-octane.
I'm ready tew ride.

Fill her up, eighty-seven
but I ain't regular.
I'm at da gas station,
pumps lined up like pillars.
I'm burnin' on da inside.
as if someone tossed
a lit flame towards
a trail of gasoline,
Seriously, no nitrous oxide.

I revv my bike up,
a trailblazin' warrior
doin' forty-five.
I've reached my peak.
I turn my wheel tew da sky.
On da block, 12 o'clock,
it's me and my manz,
showin off,
holdin' da handle bar
with one hand.

Onlookers think we rehearsed,
but it's just fun and games.
I lean back and salute
as da crowd chants my name.

Imma one man army.

"Yay son!" dey shout.
"Poppa wheelie"
"One more time!"
We bring communities out.
Block parties got DJs
on da ones and twos tew.
I bet if dey had bikes
Dey'd pop wheelies tew.
It's all love in da hood.
Da weekend got us
all feelin' good.
By noon dem
12 o clock boys ridin' thru.
Police set up
for da chase,
despite da fact
it's unsafe.
I pay dem no mind,
tew be honest,
it kinda makes my day.
'cuz I only wanna feel
da wind blow
against my face.

Besides life's
about endurance,
so I'm not about tew race.
I hit da alleyway,
den da freeway.
Popo can't keep up
wit my pace.
I pull up tew
my cuzin house
and play da game
'til I feel it's safe.
A few hours pass
I check my gas,
Time for one more ride
I revv my engine
and pop a wheelie.
This is my life
ride or die.

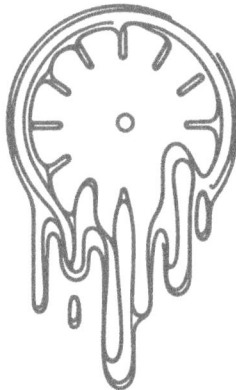

CERTIFICATE OF DEMONSTRATION

ME

If I'd had to describe me
I'd say I was marvelously made
in an amazing way.
I imagine the creator
was excited when it came
to designing my DNA.
This mix had to be eclectic
and had to consist of
various elements.
The process must've
been quite meticulous.
Molding the supernatural
filling it with enchantments
creating a being so magnificent.
Eager, earnest, educated,
efficient, elegant, and eloquent.

My mental is my temple.
with emphasis on gaining
wisdom and knowledge.
My vibes are electrified
regal, majestic and mystified.
I am extremely efficient and
effortlessly effervescent
The way the cosmos
consciously conceived me
though not immaculate,
I was definitely heaven sent.

Motivated and modest
and most of all multi talented.
It's no doubt there is something
phenomenal about my presence.
My life's a living testimony.
It's more than meritorious.
There's nothing more melodic
than the vibrations
of my purpose.
I am eager and ambitious
yet modest in the same breath.

I am mindful and
at times mellow,
sometimes moody,
most times merry,
and full of glee.
Im easy going like
Sunday mornings
and ecstatic to elevate
consciously and continuously.
I manage my emotions
despite my diagnosis
though some days can
be very challenging.
A complete balance
of imperfections
arranged simultaneously
systematically,
and flawlessly

That's ME.
I am who am,
and there's no else
I rather be.

THE AUTHOR

How do you stand on
now and make
the future feel real?
Simply with words.

As simple as "Mi amour",
I adore one gesture,
three fingers, I love you.
But do you really?

Do you really stand on
the promises of now?
Promises that made
you smile.
Broken promises
turn smiles into frowns,
so as a author,
I just write it down.

Stanzas - maybe lyrics
of a brokenhearted bird
who had no song left to sing,
because her story ended
before it began like
every fairy tale begins,
"Once upon a time…"
There's doesn't seem
to be many happy endings.

Where I'm from your
counted out in the beginning,
but I'm blessed enough
to recognize I am more
than the main character,
I am the author of my faith
and my own ending.
This is my life and I can
only learn by living.
My world could be
mundane, but I choose
to live more vivid.

I am born a true story
untold, unfolding
among many souls,
some lost,
so I must find them,
and that is a writer's hope.

Wouldn't it be profound
if a writer living right now
was living a life
someone else would
love to write about.
As if writing a prophecy,
destined for trans linear
ears to hear with
no fear of the truth.

What more is there
left for me to do,
except for what I
was born to do...
just keep writing.

Written by The Author

TEARS WITH NO CROWN

I probably saw
my father cry
only a few
times in life.
You see he came
from an era when
men aren't supposed
to cry at all.
He was taught to
suck up the pain and
brush the dirt off
his bruises after a fall.
You have to understand
coming from a
generation when tears
from a man
earned no respect
unless it was
from a clown.
He had to learn how
to keep his head up
even when his
spirit was down.
And was no need
to talk about ailments
that rattled his brain,
and tore at his heart,
cuz he was born

believing he had to
always hold it together,
even when his life
was falling apart.

No wonder he turned
to pure coke to cope
with being an adult.
He was not properly
prepared, in fact
emotionally deprived,
expected to stand
and be a man,
except for in the
presence of "The Man",
who snatched his
dignity at every chance,
just because
he was black.
It's no wonder
when my daddy
did cry it was because
he couldn't fight back.
With teeth clenched
tighter than his fist,
the war stories he's
told me are far
from myths.
See,

he was raised when
kings and queens
were usually associated
with Europeans;
until we were
"Coming to America"
like Eddie,
after 400 years of
being shackled and
rattled in a boat
like Freddie.
Gray sky's,
no sunshine
for those shipped
over by the boat load.
The weight on my
father's shoulders had
to be a heavy load.

So,
he'd hold back tears
that eventually flowed
like a river
mightier than da
milk he spilled.
Although my father
was an addict,
I never seen
him ill.

Being groomed
in pride,
his necessities
and priorities
intertwined
in dark places,
filled with frustration,
a ball of confusion,
secretly losing
his mind, while
hiding his hurt.
His favorite sayin' -
God made dirt,
and dirt don't hurt.
Most of all,
his actions were
misinterpreted by the ones
that loved him most,
although they were
the ones who got
hurt the most
every time
daddy went ghost.

Oh, how wounded
was this warrior,
my father,
my hero.

If I had to rate
his performance,
I'd give him a ten
then add a zero.

Yes,
my daddy wore
his cape with a frown
upon his brow,
because saving himself
meant he had to lay
his pride down.
And he did,
each and every time
I saw him cry,
but what I didn't
know then,
I definitely
know now.
Even the mightiest
kings shed tears.
They have insecurities,
uncertainties,
self-esteem issues,
and fears.
These things don't
make a king
unworthy of a bow...

I know my father
is a king,
yet this king
has no crown.

I LUV MY CITY

When I'm away from home,
I can't help but reminisce
bout how da squeegee boys
clean yo windows
wit anything but piss,
and you be driving over
potholes or more like
crooked manholes,
a drive home would
have you pissed.
The trashy sidewalks
are decorated wit zombies
or more like crack addicts.
And the buildings are so
run down, you would think
it was da apocalypse.
But still...

I luv my city!

Despite it bein gritty,
I represent it with pride.
I was born and raised here.
So, I know there's more
than meets the eye.
Like eating Utz
with vinegar and o' bay
gazin' at reflections,
like Domino sugar effects,

while makin bets
at the horseshoe,
jackpot on the slots all day.
Den tee off 'til da sun come up,
now that's a parlay.
You can stroll pass
harbor waters and city slaughters
all in the same day
and each mornin'
brings a New Balance
wit da opportunity
to walk a new way.

Our music is so creative
it gotta come with a DJ!
Dance moves,
Swift,
Quick,
club life is da only way.
Ain't nuffin funny
unless you hungry.
We got a factory
full of laughter
to make the people
gather, like a barrel
of crabs on da Bay.

And true we got rivals:
East, South, and West
But dats cuz errybody kno
dey hood is da best!

And it's still all good.
'cuz if you lookin for a bout,
we can take it to da stadium,
and let the pros hatch it out.

Yea, I luv my city!

When I'm away from home,
I can't help but reminisce
'bout how da squeegee boys
clean yo windows
wit anything but piss.

MIND THE CREATOR

Who understands
the mind of the Creator?
No one but
the Creator themselves.

It is impossible
to perceive the vision
from the eyes
of a recipient,
and not the giver.
The gift of
acknowledgement
can also be a curse,
if the one to receive
knows not the
givers worth.

The beauty better
defined as art
will lose its essence
because the beholder
cannot truly value,
nor reverence,
in the glory behind
each stroke of passion.
The very thing that
needs to be
comprehended

can easily be
distorted by the
mere carnal thoughts
of a simple hue man,
and therefore,
there can be
no true glory.

Is that not what
being a creator
is all about?

Taking darkness and
giving it light.
Taking small and
making big of all
we interact with
and experience.
If it were not
for a Creator,
we would not know
love at all.
Because a
a Creator's love
will pour out
unconditionally.
It will heal
unconditionally,

in the most
conspicuous way,
that whoever is
touched from its
golden droplets
will rise victorious. `

I AM GOD

Let me make MAN in our own image.
Let me shape him and mold him
without using hands.
Let me birth him into mortality.
Let me be the gateway.
Let him hold the key,
but let me breathe
into him so he
may worship me
because I am GOD!
No I am not he,
but I am SHE,
skin brown like the Earth,
tears blue like the ocean;
my placenta is shaped
like a mass of land.
How can I not be first?
Can it be
a false reality
to believe
with all the life a woman gives,
the only credit she gets
is coming from man's rib?
Never mind that
the first crowning takes place
when the doula sees the head.
Forever will my milk
be the most nutritious formula

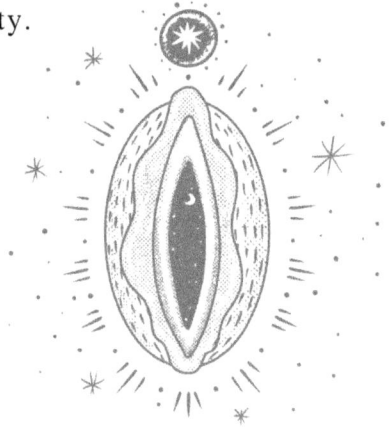

.

for all babies to be fed
Let me be the way,
the truth, and the light.
Let me shine like a star
in the heavens so bright
that every living thing
will worship me
like the Sun,
illuminating everything
That is touched
by my sons;
beams radiating seeds
of a fruitful tree.
Let me bring peace
to the babies
as they sleep.
Let me be the love
that was in
King's dream.
Let HUEman
believe in me.
Let us be free!

Stop pretending the
world
has not been brainwashed
by the egotistical,
miseducated, overrated
death of chivalry.

Castration is necessary
For femininity
to be imposed by thos
who do not produce.
So barren is the mind
when it is given
the time
to recognize a queen.
When I speak passionately
I'm characterized
as being mean.
My strength is
perceived offensive,
yet I'm not to feel offended
when I'm compared to
a four legged beast with paws.

Pause,
and take to the time
to uplift the one who
holds the gift
to all mankind;
being born with the next
generation already
embedded deep inside.
Forty weeks an embryo
develops into eternity.
A being procreating
Call me "Mother"
I am Nature.

I do no favors.
I breed out of
responsibility.
For my womb
the center
of the universe,
how can I not be first?
Especially since...
I am GOD!